subhuman.

subhuman.

POEMS

KASHAWN TAYLOR

WAYFARER BOOKS
ABIQUIU, NEW MEXICO

WWW.WAYFARERBOOKS.ORG

All Rights Reserved
Published in 2025 by Wayfarer Books
Cover Design and Interior Design by Connor Wolfe
TRADE PAPERBACK 9781965320280

10 9 8 7 6 5 4 3 2 1

Look for our titles in paperback, ebook, and audiobook wherever books are sold.
Wholesale offerings for retailers available through Ingram.

Wayfarer Books is committed to ecological stewardship.
We greatly value the natural environment and invest in conservation.

PO Box 1109, Abiquiú, New Mexico
wayfarer@homeboundpublications.com
WAYFARERBOOKS.ORG

for Kenneth Grenier

(1996 – 2024)

Contents

subhuman.

Under the Courthouse

under the courthouse
they strip you of time
of seconds and minutes
then days of your life

they strip you of you
the one you've always known
and ignore the now faceless
shell you call home

under the courthouse
everything starts to *hit*
your face burns red-hot
your mind starts to split

pacing and pacing
between future and past
how long you've been here
how if you went back

you'd make better choices
drive straight home that night
so when your eyes open
they burn bright with sunlight

not in a stuffy cell
or a dorm so minute
but this is first run
not the fucking reboot

under the courthouse
what you know is all gone
is three years enough
to fully write my wrongs?

Who Remembers Phone Numbers Anymore?

Settle down, settle down
I have moved way too much,
it has not even been
a whole month.

Don't bother making friends,
you won't be around
long enough to learn
their middle names. Be sure
to buy an address book or
rip a page from a bible
because in a few weeks,
you won't even remember
their first.

From the wild
bullpen to a dull dim
concrete room.
Moved again: a moldy
gym, then explosive East
Dorm where sneaky sickness
burrowed inside me
             — hiding! —
via the hole where my humanity
no longer resides, right
below my heart.

A quickie quarantine up the highway,
ten days in a cell,
twenty-three hours a day.
The green rubberized floor
stared back at me, welcome company.

What to do with my hour:
dial home or shower?

Settle down, settle down
I think I need to settle down.
Can you just let me settle down?
I have moved way too much,
it has not even been
a whole month—

after I have learned
          and healed
—I think my tea
kettle has settled,
my sore feet nailed
          firmly into the linoleum—anxiously

awaiting the delayed arrival
of my address book.

These Headphones Should be Free

I walk down a dim hall, and appreciate the coruscating layer of wax on the floor

(how I could sleep there!)

laid probably earlier today, or last week, or in the time before Securus tablets, that time before headphones when Jesus Christ himself roamed old earth and pulled men

from dirt slumber. Why are you complaining? It is unbecoming and very much beneath you, very much like the man you ran into the soil, velvet sky polka-dotted with the remnants of creation winking overhead. He'll never

listen to *The Trouble with Fever*, and would never ever stew over a lack of cheap earbuds. Even that, I am certain, is beneath him.

I aspire to be more like that man. Quiet, cold, painless, alone. Instead, The Man gave me everything to which I am entitled: purple and turquoise walls, three hots, a cot, and Scantron grocery lists. Among other things, I am filled to the brim with privilege; the sum of thirty-six months is mercy. Divine. Ineffable. Using a borrowed black

Bic I bubble off what, by chance or by karma, I am missing, bite my tongue till it bleeds, and swallow copper self-righteousness and leaden pride. Force myself to

remember how life is unfair, how one life snuffed out becomes many, and how much money I'll have for next week's order. I imagine in vivid phantasmagoria how different life might be if I paid attention in church, if I kept on going every Sunday with Grandma. Probably I'd still be an erupting volcano of shame and contrition, wondering forever

where Jesus Christ is when you need him and whether my prayers are just mp3s for aliens.

Theoretical Math for DOC Employees

If the prison is down
sixteen counselors
with only three supervisors,
then the sum of frustration
must surely be greater
than or equal to all
vacation days taken
when our livelihoods
are at stake.

However:
if certain conditions
aren't met, that is,
enough officers
to be let out for rec,
the square root
of our dignity multiplied
by the collective indolence
—nine times out of ten—
equals funereal impatience
tangible in my dorm.

It is *quite* simple.
The number of supercilious answers
given to heart—
burning questions is just
a sand-grain percentage of the superfluity
their words carry.

And if you can't wrap
your head around this:
shut up,
        and sign up for school.

The Bathroom Just Smells Better During Late Night, Okay?

at last!
I topple off
my bunk, shh!
dorm quiet
a mouse
scurries by
say hi! to Mr. Jingles
the big screen
television playing
SNL while C.O.
whatshisface
shouts no! in his sleep
it feels wrong
      an arrant aberration
to empty my bladder
its 3am—
the smell of swill
dutifully removed hours
ago, the community
sump smells fresh!!
      like disinfectant,
that is. lemon scented
spray because bleach,
They say, is much
too urbane
I hope I hope
no one wakes
when worms gambol about
those ptomaine shower drains

or when the toilets flush
it's just so messy
when the sun's around
& when it's down
my bunkie isn't nodding
off at urinals
       spraying!
dubious fluids on the floor
it's just *so* messy
when the sun's

               around.

Where's the Mail?

O' joyous Monday!
Weekends inside are inedible:
Saturday tough chewing,
a steak too well done,
rib way past its prime,
and Sunday solid
like a lumpy sack of old
potatoes begging to be mashed.
My weekends:
brake-pad meatloaf cooked
twelve minutes too long,

sludge gravy golden brown
a mouthful of seawater—
toxic, harmful bodies.
On weekends, all movement ceases,
messenger doves with word
of how freedmen progress
    or regress
refuse to rest wing and dine here,
knowing better than to risk
losing their little bird brains.

How times have changed,
anticipating Monday's first
buttery light; it is ready
to be devoured whole, rich
flaky crust and sweet
sweet filling smackdab in
the middle of forty-eight
abominable hours marked
by patience, suffering.

Lessons in Cell Etiquette

The strange man sleeping
in the strange land beneath mine
casts his line into the dark
trying to catch my sex

His interrogatives grope & prod
are slippery avaricious fingers
fingering for what he's missed
these last precious four years

on time out from the world
looking to pilfer what he needs
and entomb in his mind
for three final years my sex

then continue bruising until bored
At some point my act
of altruism slides downhill
becomes a parasitic felony

unfettered taking
I handed him tiny wet
fragments of me willingly
they are all I have

to trade for shards of peace
Generosity is a gift of the rich
I am without employ
tender body as body tender slow

I give in   slippage
on my knees rubbed raw
his pick smashing blindly
at numb desensitized ice

fishing for my sex
I am used to this   expended
but this time I swear
is always the last time

What he took satisfied a need
biological and acceptable
by some old laws when
the fairer body is unavailable

                    Feeling emptied he'll never know
                    I keep my sex in a different hole

Old Light

Remembering in chains is light years;
it is viewing the past
through a priceless telescope,
how you remember the last
time your eyes met, each wrinkle
tattoo, scar, missing tooth,

how you remember his fist
or her lips or that hole
in the drywall of the bedroom
put there by a manic
combination of passion and punishment

unchanging, obdurate

the last vestiges and testimony
of the ever-expanding space
between two bodies.

Light years are hard, reliable.
Memory, however, may shape the future.
No matter the frequency of our light,
no matter how new the lens
through which we look
or how many expensive mirrors affixed to telescopes
nothing will change the fact:
We live the past in perpetuity—
time flows on.

And memory, like how we perceive
primordial first galaxies born
                    after Big Bang,

is just old light.

Subscribe to Read the Whole Story, or Headline Hoarders

tap tap tap
this tablet, an overpriced brick
a pitiful panacea for rotten foundations

we can't do news oh no
you cannot do news
unless your pockets are stuffed
       or your life support bleeds money

so maybe the world ends
too preoccupied to notice
trying to power past headlines

those things, lying like rugs
mendacious and misleading—
what is the point of forever scrolling?
       an appearance of progressive prisoning

please, help me buy
the thirteen-inch clear TV
the man inflates four times the cost

because yes that's the best
use of the government change Grandma
spares on me the 3rd of each month;
       not ramen but outside information

so when the bombs drizzle
from Los Angeles to Times Square
I'll forever have Fox News

on my hi-def idiot tube,
a pleasant distraction
from the distant sound
      of freedom beginning to ring

Of Giving Up

"If your compassion does not include yourself, it is incomplete."
–Jack Kornfield

It's 6:27am. Bathroom.
Sleep, like a trembling kitten,
eluded me last night.
Like nights before.
In that way, sleep
is like peace.
The plastic funhouse mirror
reflects giving up—
ghastly fluorescent light magnifies
squalor in my long face,
the lines drawn by pissing
8 months' worth of fucks
down clogged communal toilets.
I finger the new dark acne
scar—a jagged line—zigzagging
my corrugated forehead just
above my right eyebrow.
The product of giving up.
Gently tracing its rough ridges,
I remind myself to live
and—

—desperate coughing grates
my ears, the sound yellow-green-brown,
the sound phlegm, bubonic.
Like a flash of slow lightning,
I think: if it is plague, dying

among this sacrilegious chorus
of congestion is fine.
Just fine.

Back in the mirror.
It is *all* for me.
A hint of eucalyptus rises
from a travel-sized container,
familiar royal blue.
The smell of Grandma Rose,
the wrinkles on her face, hands
like a sagacious grape,
years in the sun.

Commissary Cuisine Art

gas station food
arrives Wednesday morning
here in J-Dorm and,
in the bustling night,
the gelatinous stench
poisons our dead air.
microwave fried
                    processed meats
(chorizo // turkey sticks // hot beef)
instant rice—
white and its more specific
sophisticated orange cousin,
Spanish—and wraps craftily
created with crumpled Doritos.

trades:
Maruchan Ramen Noodles
tantamount to cinnamon raisin
bagel or a half-bag of
Velveeta cheesy refried beans.
Dunkin sticks! what are …
          those?
Bait fish fried in soybean
oil, because we're prey now.

an advertisement—BIG MEALS!
now: 40% less sodium,
but the salt still stings
my surly eyes or
perhaps it's my greasy heart
refusing to beat on
or just maybe!
it's my enraged stomach
begging to be sated
with real food.

Hard Work

The water cooler
looks mighty different
these days: chilly

lidless steel seat,
walls just over my waist, doors
a thin swinging censor
bar, so gazes meet and fleet;
aromas comingle circumspectly
to show proper respect to those
already working, a
coterie of fetidness, eau de
effluvium, before clocking
in for a new day of hard work.

My colleagues rotate monthly,
turnover rate egregious like the sounds
which ricochet like bullets
in a bank vault
off these shared walls and harass
my nose. Was that a duck
or a raspberry, a machine gun?
I did not ask to be killed
or fucked today.
That they leave so quickly,
like summer winds, does not impede
company progress—we lumber
on, but they always come back,
bloodshot eyes, missing teeth,
exploded capillaries, ethanol breath.

Shame lives here
no longer, only running
showers and whooshing toilets,
a noxious humidity coating my skin
and, not least of all,
a gut-wrenching sense of hot urgency
stabbing my bowels which screams
You're well past the deadline!
Please, evacuate!

My concentration wavers.
Not emails or micromanagers,
but loquacious coworkers;
a gossamer palaver
forces my intestines into turtle torpidity
as we race toward shared goals.

God, grant me
a crumb of comfort,
some scruples of peace, a
semblance of solitude
as beads of salty sweat
—or maybe they're tears—
sting my eyes, dot my thighs
and splash into the toilet bowl.

Meditation on Trying to Obtain the Typewriter

We are forgotten ink.
Culture buried deep
beneath mounds of paper
working to gasp for air;
voices ragged with decades
of silence, coated in ashes—
the men and women of yore
both intrepid and elegiac
blotted indelible tales on ancient
parchment begging the masses

remember us
we are (were) people too
we *exist(ed)*

We are pecuniary hallucinations.
Raffish carrion immortalized
as characters in books, on screens
big blows to budgets, a waste
we *waste*—our legacy
as progressive beings:
waste.
Watch our lips working,
pink vocal chords stretching,
ready to give impassioned inculcation.
Our reticence imposed by generational fear.
Power to shatter sound barriers:
        the importance of being silenced.

Lamentations

We found our rodent
friend in a cobwebbed corner
by empty lockers, black
eyes frozen open in
abject terror. I swear
one eye twitched a morose
pleading glance: *help me*.
How I wished to perform
crude surgery, plastic spork
for lack of smart silver scalpel,
scoop out Mr. Jingles's wide
lifeless eyes and peer into
his obsidian orbs, relive
the terrors of his last
gargantuan moments
seared into his retinas
because those old-timey doctors
only thought they were wrong.
That farfetched hypothesis:
eyes take a final snapshot
        before death.

Dressed in grand cerements,
one-ply toilet tissue and rough
handkerchiefs, our whiskered
boy prepared to depart
down that slick steel
swirl, cushioned by lead
water. Communal bathroom

sweetened with mourning,
defecation, and religious
oils spritzed from recycled
nasal spray bottles.
Does anyone have any last
words for Mr. Jingles, last
of his order, first of DOC?
Forever: one of us.

A Proper Shower

1.

First, you must disinfect
the correct stall,
which everyone agrees
is the second to last
on the right. The water
pressure is two-star-hotel,
and *that* is saying something.
In lieu of scrubbing
with the frayed long-handled brush
I opt for double-fisting
dueling spray bottles
electric green for all-purpose
pale yellow Lemonal to remove
just some of the rinsed-off regrets
of the man who washed before me.

My sanitary reverie is stolen
away when the liver-spotted man
undressing to my right speaks:
That's a great idea.
Yeah, I guess it is.

2.

Once stripped to unmentionables
you must make a grave choice:
wash your shame by hand
or entrust it with biweekly laundry.
I choose the latter,
because it has been a soiled year.
All the fucks I once gave

about scratchy shitty underwear live
in the shower drain with black maggots.
My fucks smell larval, of rotten
hair, dead skin, and, of course, lemon.

3.

To start this cleaning ritual
there is a circular bit
of raised metal which one
must not press exactly,
but must apply a slight pressure.
It takes a moment to register
touch like an old cellphone
or a penis that's been gripped
too tightly for too long
by pruned hands which feel
all too familiar, but which are all one has.

There is no temp
control, so I pray the water
will bake me this time.
I am afraid the hot or cold
depends on where the sun hangs
in New England's sky or how I feel.
I never thought to ask.
Well, I cannot feel the sun
and I hang desperate,
one of many stray dogs begging
for scraps and good fortune.
I sigh at my funhouse reflection

in the lustrous silver tomb
& press the button.
The water glacially impales my body
(butsweetdeathdoesnotcome)
like I belly
flopped from ten stories high
onto a frozen motel pool.

4.

If you dissociate, you may,
for a time, elude all stress:
that felonious fear of forever
being a second-class citizen
which re-dawns every so often
mid-sentence, like the slowest strike
of toxic lightning; ruminations
over the ever-changing world,
what you missed, what and whom
you will never get back.

As the water hydrates my kinks,
beads on my stomach and ass,
my dick refuses to cooperate.
Under normal circumstances
I'd use my left, as though my cell
were in my right, scrolling.
But if I turn my head
at the wrong moment, eyes
might meet with meat in hand,
and that is *not* normal,
so I switch to my right.
A stranger is stroking me.
I am almost there.

Good Idea Man starts harmonizing
with the patter and sputter of water;
euphoria escapes me despite
my tender stranglehold.
Back to the flaccid beginning.

5.

Before you exit and enrobe
you must lather, rub, wash, and rinse.
I suggest you repeat and repent.

I am clean, but I am not
in the mood to experience,
to be experienced.
There is a delicate layer of scum
I cannot quite see, but feel,
can never abrade. Other
hawkeyed men, however, can
see something is awry, squalid.
As I pat dry my brown back,
shoulders, they see real filth.

Maybe it's the hard water
or unfinished prurient thoughts.
Is what they see my hope
crushed under a conviction?
I need another shower.
Wet filth is still filth, after all.

The Altar

She operates on Fridays
in shadows and venom
Things she carries:
a title—counselor supervisor;
a smile and compassion
clean manufactured, the product
of what the Department calls

education

I call it: rehearsal

Sure, we were three
but it was all about me,
the *other* other, an outcast
in a swarm of degenerates,
the bee in a nest of hornets

I sat dumbfounded
                    —jawdropped!—
eyes narrowed in my seat,
library still dark, uninviting
is that how you see me?

Unworthy

of fluorescent light, the saddest
variety, the least flattering.
Perhaps she knew:
once illuminated, virulence
withers and dies

Her fangs struck quick, precise
Our lighthouse smiles reduced to
flirtation, our innocent intimacy

  inappropriate

Parroting distorted perceptions
she cannonballed threats to divide

                              and thus (never) conquer!

based on fabricated transgressions
invented by those for whom change
breeds fear, the unknown unholy

My friends are good men—
their eyes saw through the guise,
beheld the feeble crux
of our prejudiced predicament:
our camaraderie doomed them,
made them bleating lambs
already at the altar

                                        mid-slaughter

and fate forced me to watch
them squirm and cry, bleed out
their reputations scarlet-stained
before our black-clad uniformed
executioners trained indoctrinated axes

                                        at my neck.

                    //

Not for the first time
I found myself on my knees
arms out in supplication
apologizing to straight men,

for their kindness and friendship
invariably causes psychic violence
Because that's the way it is

                                                 How dare I

risk connection in chains?

                                                 How dare I

think it cool to emulate
mirth, card games, normality?

                                             To appropriate it

all for my own—I am
criminal. How dare I?

She silenced my voice,
knocked me with her stiff authority
to the ground and when I tried

                                          to stand tall again

she placed her badge just above
the small of my back

                                                I crumbled

like paper in frustrated writer hands
but would not allow the salty
satisfaction of tears.

                              //

The air still thick
with hearsay and sweat
I demanded an audience

                                          for my pain

and she reminded

is everything
except for my perception of bigotry, of pitchfork hate
Is it not easy to take
such a stance, maybe my past
distorted my reality?
She bit, rivulets of red
clear poison coating bared teeth
She asked why
Why was I the advocate,
where were my friends?
She was

                                                      not blind

her blue eyes lightning
but refused to see

What I understood:
the faggot must navigate
a minefield balancing on fragile
lines, must be miserable,
an unhinged solitary creature

                                       of lust, of madness

This *is* prison, a punishment
after all

                        //

A thing or two
I know for sure:
to love and be loved

                                            is not a crime

& the malfeasance occurred
not between our paroxysms of laughter,
it found haven with her in

                                        administrative darkness,

a lack of paperwork:
a parasitic, pervasive culture of

                                    intolerance & victim blaming

She was right,

                It needs to stop.

Black Enough

Whether I wear
my hair in hurried cornrows
or set it free, unleashed
a stormy crown of coils
divine nappy halo
framing my brown face
I may never be black enough

Even if I am resigned
when men with skin the color of my palms
reach out from behind me
cop their furtive feels, and I laugh
at their theft, the violation
        or
If I only smile and drag my feet onward
when the blonde buxom third shift cop
compares my divinity to steel wool
I may never be black enough

The elegant way my tongue dances
behind full lips and words
cascade clearly past the slight
gap between my front teeth
breeds no confusion
that I am not black enough

The proof secreted in how
I say *ask* and not *aks*
how my ostentatious degrees radiate
from my grandma's living room wall.
& how I choose not to reclaim

that slur in casual conversation
unless a fire within me screams
—just cause!—
tells you that
I am not black enough

When my brothers from the hometown
aks about the sounds in my ear
or if I have seen this movie or that,
they referencing that ubiquitous binary:
        black or white
                (right or wrong)
because in their eyes, the same
survival brown as mine,
I cannot just be me,
emotional and cocoa-butter soft.

subhuman.

A Face in Judgment

(after Devin Odell's essay of the same name)

Marco

in all his various incarnations,
hues of flesh
and constituent parts

is thriving.

He has three kids
with two women, a job—
not a great job, but a good job
that toughens his tanned hands,
keeps the lights glowing,
the shower flowing,
and pays most all the bills
which stack on an old table
in, I guess, what one might call
"the dining room"
of his ramshackle apartment
just outside the heart
of his inner-city hometown
which he will never escape.

If speculation, desires,
fears and values decide
brown and Black futures, then maybe
Mercy should have something to do with it.
But judges are the old gods,

the real heroes and villains,
all in the same black lachrymal costume
                    (impossible to determine
who is which!),
who hand clean pristine slates & chances
to white youth after white youth
who are soso sorry, again
Iamsosorry,
time and time again,
the sorriest thing in the room.

Judge,
I am not requesting a defense, or
even explanation of your decisions,
I am asking you,
in your dark nimbus robes,
set high above the courtroom,
to remember the future
and denounce what the past
so often dictates when you face
Marco's baby cousin
as the second or third hearing,
bright and much too early on tomorrow's docket.

Excuse me: I may not be worthy
            unqualified to speak
& it is difficult, I know, to
root yourself in our real reality,
to climb down from Olympus's thin-air apogee and consider
our faces, beautiful with melanin and broad noses,
just might be equal to yours in value,
our minds and lives Rubik's-cube complex.

Marco said *I'm scared.*
Scared for real.
But he escaped, not ensnared
for life by a maligned machine,
a system that forgets
you exist once judgment is passed.
There is no rule.

Your next Marco might not
be so lucky, and *these facts matter.*
He, too, will be repentant on his knees
—soso sorry!—
and scared, scared for real
and will demand emotional eye contact,
human attention from the human scale
which weighs his worth.

You didn't know about Marco
or how his life pulsed on,
and I hope it sparks joy
like Fourth of July fireworks
                    (God… bless America.)
to know he's alive.
You have a mouthful of questions,
        I'm sure,
but Marco's doing just fine.

Almost Sonnet for the Life I Almost Lived

A heart that knows my agony
Cannot make that pain unknown
I lie in mental atrophy
I feel the weight of time alone
A dream of worlds I cannot bear
An endgame eyes just can't perceive
I've lived a life beyond repair
That life I only wish to leave
    So I pen poems, stories, letters
    Things more fit to endure time better

Sunset, 7 April 2023

The sky outside is cotton candy.
Streaks of sugar-blue clouds
weaving through lightning pink
strands of firmament.
He called me from bed
to view—and without doubt,
I am glad of it.
I've not observed nature,
been touched by puckish green
blades of grass or eloped
in sprawling, verdant wood
in too many days to count.
But surely, a gentle breeze,
wistful and reminiscent of gumdrops,
would brush my born-again virgin nose, light
and wonderful. The sun,
it's setting, and I hunger to taste the fading capacious
violent peach-pink sky. For dessert,
I'll devour the rich blackness
dividing the stars.

Begging

(for Bobby)

bruised skinned bloody
knees always betray
steel face and mission-
statement gait, because
in your freedom
there is power over me;
I, forced to rely on you,
my need incremental
pours down on you torrential
eroding what was once
concrete solid
until the remains are sediment
and I, corrosive—please,

pick up the phone.

Hot Water Blues

Why argue with the old man
who left the hose
connected to the mop sink
running running running?
No guarantees or icy promises;
the hot water might be gone forever.

My counselors preach forgiveness,
how essential it is for healing.
Don't you think, they counsel,
frigid liquid might mend
the crack bifurcating your heart?
Or, at the very least,
learn you a gelid lesson
in culpability and humility?

The clenched fist of an incensed lover,
a shivery strip search by the Handoflaw,
the cool kiss from the barrel of a gun,
                    or the artic drip
of dry dry water after a hard
long day of prisoning:
always take what you can get.
My counselors?
                    The best I can get.

When the polar shock subsides,
when my frosty breath returns, and I
             feel subzero and invigorated,
maybe I will consider chilly forgiveness.
Maybe I can start,
however infinitesimal,
with the bastard who
jacked the hot water.

Sad Fruit

Apples here taste so bitter,
copper, like chewing a battery
or a secret lover's bottom lip;
angry apples, determined to,
at the same time,
nourish and punish.
I imagine the destitute orchard
from which they come,
the desperate trees on which they grow.
How the soil might taste
if I consumed a moist, grainy handful,
broke my teeth on stones
and the bones of small animals
cursed to rest in the eldritch pasture.
Would my roots wither,
become petrified tendrils, arms
fingering for loamy sustenance?
Would my trunk grow strong,
a redoubtable oaken bulwark,
or would it fail, and fall
like the Wall in its sole task?
Could my leaves withstand the gale,
the fusillade of rain, the sunshine-
joy and two AM-doom of summer?

//

My bark yearns
to be hugged before nuclear
autumn, before small animals shelter
and the birds ride prevailing winds south.

If there was a little love,
the raven smoke from these fires
which choke and erase
might give birth to new beginnings,
a phoenix-resurrection for
the sad fruit I give to this sad world.
It is true:
our roots dictate our growth,
but even those can be excavated,
then replanted.
It is our seeds which float
the lightest breeze, that roam
farther than our dying, browning
leaves and leave flavors
—bitter or sweet?—
on the puckered lips of lives
we never come close to kissing.

Shambles!

After learning the news,
Lucien grew hot
& fell mute,
closed his heavy eyes,
and shivered in his dreams,
thinking there'd be no tomorrow.
The next morning
the sun rose in the east,
as it always does,
roaring into space
its silent radioactive scream,
and he lamented his tainted blood
to his sister and to me,
a stranger delivered to him
by shit luck and circumstance—
the only sympathetic ear
in a microcosmic cacophony of 100 men.
He conflated sex with love,
dreaded the conversations
which must now take place
on a prison payphone
while he pretended to be strong,
knowing that if his voice cracked
even once, the whole world
might shatter again.
Don't ignore the science
I said and I told him
I loved him and I did,
in the way one loves another
human being when they hurt,
when they need a Band-Aid

on their heart and all
you have is kindness.
Lucien went about his tomorrow,
only a bit less radiant
than the sun,
with which he wanted to scream
into space for humanity
to bear witness to his plight.
He searched forever
seeking those pieces of himself
washed away like a drop
of viral blood in water, wondering
how fundamentally life can change
yet remain the same.

A Plane Coming in For Landing at Bradley International Airport

To be an insect
in the recreation yard:
life buzzing past, fast
nipping at society's ear
swatted into submission by
the pale uneven Handoflaw.

Multitudinous in number,
we gather when sun is high,
heat and rays strongest—a ritual
feast: salvaged hope, scraps!—
and vibrate as a hive, one
whole. Can you hear us

pleading with beating wings
frantic and kamikaze dives
down defenseless throats?
Blacks and browns, greens,
red. Our sizes, shapes, our faces
run one side of the gamut—

we all carry the same insignificance from the sky.

Salvador :(

!!!what a mess!!!

I had my glasses on
the whole entire time,
walking with the sun
burning my back—
so you know that I could see

yet somehow I still fell
into this pit, a trap
          and BOY!
am I falling still, the light
at the apogee of this vertical tunnel
growing smaller and smaller,
a needlepoint of ultraviolet hope,
less reachable, my end becomes
more palpable in groves

on the way
down,
I think of how strong
my arms are; if I can
climb my way back up…
on the way
down,
I notice this black well is slick,
oiled up so no hope may
snake its way from bottom to top.
I can only pray
the bottom is lined
with red cushions,
heart-shaped pillows and a knife.

On the Utility of Phone Socks

There are secrets
privy only to the coarse fibers
of designated phone socks,
whims whispered by rattling tongues
to indifferent lovers cuddled in bed
with their own warmer lovers,
words warbled with savior intention
though the notes fall flat
                    fall hard
and die, consumed by static obsolescence.

Love, it seems, becomes muffled
        by phone socks:
cotton-mouthed chatter
redolent of corn chips;
army of fuzzballs buzzing
with romance, they are bleach sharp
        in predator formation
primed to snap at the jugular.

If I used a phone sock,
I'd choose one fresh from the package
without holes,
which is to say my words
would be kept safe
never allowed to seep
into air, like lead into water;
my words would bake, sweat
sounds like bodies coming together
under covers, stifled cries
of ecstasy or for help!

Without phone socks,
love sounds suspiciously like rabid anger.
My demands for attention,
wild-eyed surprise that time
in fact flowed forward without me,
that you're a new father
that she is now married

that I am not a star

this world is not my solar system
but my gravity is immense, my
force a wrecking ball

a verity as rude and jagged
as the words hissing from my mouth
untampered and raw, unprotected
no glove   all love

the truth is rock-hard
phone socks are necessary

Little Cup

(for Kenny)

Awake before the sun,
I fill the little white cup
you gifted me in parting
last night with freeze-dried
Colombian instant coffee,
the aroma robust and earthy and South American
        exotic.
The dusty vents spew ice this morning.
I shake, and I spill
powdery white creamer along
its chilly lip, on the dull tile floor.
Leave the taste of French vanilla
       for the ants today.

My resealable bag of cappuccino
crinkles between slender brown fingers
rippling from my locker
throughout the dorm, tickling
sleeping ears. I pause.
Scoop.

Red safety lights glow ominously overhead,
a tenebrous warning:
pivot! you are alone now,
as I tap the steel nozzle.
I hiss, pull back for it is hot,
ripe for the taking like the old
blankets discarded on your bunk,
browned with stray coffee.
I drown the mixture in steaming

water and it, like us, becomes
changed entirely—a mélange
both congenital and external.

On my way back,
I pause, look left.
Your empty bunk jars me;
I expect your body like a felled tree
in the sad space you called home.
Both hands wrapped
tightly around your little white cup,
I cherish its newfound warmth
tempered by insipid chestnut-stained plastic.

There is no mattress
no body nobody
no scattered belongings
hanging haphazardly from the tray up top.
There is only me, an eddy
of snores, and this little cup.
I snap on the pale red sip-lid,
slide white latch open. Scent sighs
into the air, cloying and nostalgic
and like you leaving,

inescapable. I sip.

III.

(*after Mary Oliver and MARINA*)

1.

Wrapped neatly,
loosely, tied delicately
with light white yarn
and smoky gloom heavy,
I peered down intently
into the tiny box filled
with starving darkness Leo presented

last Fourth of July.
How fitting, reasonable,

thoughtful

to gift plain death to loved
ones, seasoned with ascetic apology
marinated all spring in whiskey
and cocaine, on Independence Day.

(God... bless America!)

2.

I jumped in...
        deep.
Fleshy feast for lustrous
thick black. Ignominy aside—
vast emptiness is fecund
obdurate   voracious.

Loquacious and soporific
its tendrils are congenital
ardent like dormant viral
infection. A cake walk:
to be human. The box is a gun.

3.

Food for maudlin white flowers.
We, the leftovers, often querulous.
Through the lachrymal fog—
its ossified fingers both searching
       & guiding—
mewls a fatherless cherub
pink   vulnerable   sibylline
coddled in soft expansive darkness
the fastidious gray specter of death
      —miasmic in his ubiquity,
his effrontery redoubtable—
howls in cold wind.
In dewy grass: neonatal innocence.

The most prudent use of sorrow:
     to love recklessly.

I'm Happy for You, Really

When I asked my cousin
Isaac to reach into our shared
past and pluck you
from partisan peace/manufactured obscurity
so I could compare our presents,

I imagined you'd come
kicking and screaming
as though it were my bed again,
my sheets and our sweat
binding us together
while you were on the run
from the Law and from that scared
sliver of you that needed me.
Or, just maybe, you'd come
kicking and screaming
like your six-year-old son
that day I drove us to the park,
and he pitched an all-mighty tantrum,
throwing himself into the moist
pasture behind the baseball field,
painting the new shirt and sneakers
        for which I paid
something like dirty-money green.
Like father, they say.

But instead you came
without fuss or pomp. Maybe
you came sadly, and that's fair.
It's how I've chosen to remember
your coming, anyway.

Now you live by the waves
with your girlfriend,
one with water every day.
As we spoke, a foamy tide
lapped longingly at your ankles,
at my eager ears, and the sand
between your toes, underfoot
crackledcrunched   grated
like nails on a broken blackboard
in a desolate school in my mind.
A place I never thought I'd return to
willingly ever again.

Your new girl, who is not me,
is not the one
we used to abandon those nights
you were a fugitive and slept
in woods under trees over leaves under stars
or that one instance
cuddled in a tent in my back yard,
those same nights we sighed secrets
sealed with Natty Daddies and semen.

You don't drink anymore.
It's been better than a year.
I'm happy for you, really,
but you are not so special.
I, too, have denounced liquid poison,
though under sadder circumstance.
Still, it remains all I have:
Where's my fucking trophy?

Look at you: not quite weatherman-
plain, but unseasoned chicken nonetheless.
There are beaches the world over,
and I can build my own
—a dirty beach is still a beach!—
but I think I might love you
or want to be you or need
one more chance to demolish you
before our connection severs
for good, and I end this call.
I think you might love me

and that is not fair
because there is no future
in my future; with no money
I can breathe pleasures
not even your girlfriend
              or the sea
can dream up.

Before you turned yourself in
we lay naked and drunk
on my ravaged bed. The room,
I am sure, smelled of aroused
trees in summer. We held
no pretense of modesty,
never had a need for masks.
There was a queer beauty
in how natural we were,
how primitive it felt
to *become* together.

It's been better than a year
but you answered in two rings
and said: *I stole your destiny.*
You reminded me of that October
night where I traced your tattoos
with tongue tip and you mused

"You must find a way
to win with the hand
life deals you."

Then, I said nothing,
too busy internalizing
the lines of your thighs,
but I might have agreed.
Now, rotting behind the same
walls where you experienced *Revival!*
I demand a new deal.

I Disorganize the Books

on the sagging bookshelf
because I suffer
daily from impostor syndrome.
This is not who I am,
what I am meant to be.
This life was a sink hole
into which I fell, out
of which there is no
escape, and so I smile
        —show teeth!—
shake hands, say yes,
offer to do finger-cramping
tedium, that blundering
busywork because although
I am, on the outside,
ostensibly whole, underneath
the weary worn cloudy veneer,
I am held together
with cheap Scotch tape
whose sad glue is deteriorating
and fast.
My need of disorder
cannot be coaxed or counseled
from the black creases of my mind,
but I have Time
to figure this all out and what is
Time if not grandiose compassion
fatigue? And so I place
Baldaccis between ousted Kings,
spread Evanovich's vast numbered rainbow
across the rows to live

crooked and unneatly
among tattered ancient Pattersons,
jaundiced Connellys and Cusslers,
coverless Johansens donated
with godly intention by Sister Jerilyn
all to quell a raging tornado
ravaging the electric ecosystem
from floor to lofty gray canopy
that is my mind. A lesson
in controlled chaos.

Basically a Psychologist

Again I had the dream
where I was naked, erect,
baking store-bought chocolate
chip cookies, the rusty gas
oven plugged merrily in to nothing.

If you want to chop it up,
says Jill the Social Worker,
I can lend an ear or two—
don't use them, don't need them.

But first I must disgorge
the raw air I ingurgitated
on the pilgrimage to her office.
It prickles my tongue, cheeks:
its freshness is volatile,

corrosive like bleach and ammonia,
or nitroglycerin. But this, and
the fact that her office lies
just beyond one remotely

locked door and down a hall
about twelve yards, is out
of my control. If I were mindful,
I'd *let it go*,
but I am mindless—

it resides in the distant past,
shrouded like a reaper
in a dense fog, rose-colored nostalgia.

I am hindered gravely
by hindsight, I'm afraid.

She suggests yoga, guided
meditation. To live presently
in the present. I raise
my arms, show her:

rigid, inflexible. Instead,
I suggest a teardrop
tattoo. To remember the life
I mourn nightly on my knees.
There I go again!

Put that thing on a leash,
she says, and I hallucinate it,
not pink, but bleeding gray, dripping red
trying and failing to escape

her office, but that's wistful
thinking. I'd do better to roll
up my dusty psych degree,
set fire to one end, and prescribe myself
exercise and excessive masturbation.

Meditation on Trying to Obtain the Typewriter

We are forgotten ink:
Arbitrary blots of toner
printed on bright recycled paper,
ordered and delivered
with the press of a button
by counselors whose eyes roll
liked marbled bowling balls
when we approach with smiles
and questions, whose precise aim
knocks us down—STRIKE!—
and despite incipient strength,
we remain unable to stand,
guttered.

I asked to hammer
my voice into history
with STRIKE! after STRIKE!
of key after key
so that my progeny remembers

I am(was) a person, too
I *exist(ed)*

The machine collected dust
as we collect crumbs of hope:
slowly   slowly   slowly
until what's accumulated
shrieks for attention,
voice ragged with sores, scores
of disuse misuse, no longer afraid
of the Handoflaw, the whip.

Maybe we and the obsolescence
are one and the same,
destined to STRIKE! fear
into hearts of Captains, Wardens
          unless for legal use only;

destined to be ignored,
sequestered in a bleak corner
of life's backroom for fear of exposure.
Courage to demand and command
          light:
the importance of being silenced.

15-Minute Love

Sitting cooly between us
in your idling car,
there is a warm pestilence;
a taciturn gray-pale memory
of a phallus-shaped ghost
both connects and divides
us, as we pierce night,
gunmetal Cadillac a bullet
weaving sleekly slickly through black
deserted city streets.
There is unspoken need.
I don't call you

anymore, for you love attention
and, for you, my love comes
from pity, that deep clench-cramp
white-hot forever
in my cavernous stomach.
You quaked

with my lips wrapped sycophantic
around the only body
part from which you glean gilded worth.
Gluttonous, I ate well.
You'd have soft fists,
full testicles without me.

//

Right now, she's probably riding
that screeching slug, hips
pistoning, bucking like some
foaming rodeo bull, voices entwined
sick rapture! a two-man choir
named Desire while her child
giggles petulantly from the pew.

Left on the side
of the road, pewter plumes
from the exhaust searing my throat,
staining my eyes, because
all I have left to give:
time in fifteen-minute recorded intervals.

I don't call you;
I remember, however. Yes, I
recall, as do you, the shudders,
how I run deep,
an umbral esophageal cave,
the heat, your fingers in my hair,
oh! the heat, white-hot finale
                              (gluttonous!).

All this, brushing the back
        of my tongue.

The Long Business of Dying

You never owned a suit, so you wore new blue jeans and a black t-shirt.

For some it's instant, as painless as exhaling heavy July air. For others—for you—it is a years' long affair. For all it is transactional.

Bartering. Back and forth, a tottering dance, seduction suffered in silence.

Courtship. It was in your genes.

That first meeting pulled you under. Morbidity never stopped death; it basked in the slow crawl. A razor in hand, you shaved off pieces of yourself with each line, looking for *that* feeling again, until so little of you remained even breathing became a burden.

//

Peace was afoot, and you were so sorry sitting alone in your car at Holiday Inn, your ID placed neatly on the dashboard. So sorry, but you had to do it. And, because death gets to have all it wants, you went into that final meeting wearing what you always wore, and sealed the deal—a lifetime

in the making!—by closing your eyes and letting us go.

Hello, I am Not a Murderer

With those sacred words
          and proffered hand
I will introduce my new
self to the new world,
as though I am a newborn,
drunk on innocence
afraid of bright lights
a tumultuous life
and rummaging through the thick
rheumy haze of public opinion

When news broke on social media
          they dropped me
as though I were catching:
an infection with heart,
the question of soul remains unanswered
          they dropped me
as though my acquaintance radiated
sour-green rays of contagia
and any proximity
by wire or satellite or blood
would spell Chernobyl for their reputation

Hello, I am not a murderer,
you cannot deny,
is, at the very least, catchy
Not like the four-four beat
of the latest jam smashing
the charts and the radio
or that new BK burger jingle
haunting the crevice between

          your eyes
but more like bees—
buzzworthy   painful   essential

When news broke on social media
Eric sent me a clear message:
Hey killer!
and to feel the weight of those words
I swallowed my phone
as though it were him again
breathless, moaning my name
in the front seat of my wrecked Jeep

That black curse of knowledge,
an incurable voracious cancer
devouring equally both the knower
                    and the known
A shared tumor, etiology unknown, invades
not the soft tissue of the brain
but the mind and feeds
                    (gluttonously)
on sweet cloying conviction

With those hallowed words
                    and a dollop of super glue
I will fashion flimsy lead armor, smile
                    (show teeth!)
and laugh at jokes, lame and dead as starlight,
take the world's rejection
back arched, like a fucking man
while my phone festers and churns
vibrating *buzz buzz* in my stomach.

A Personal History of Violence

Growing up, I was a vacation
home. Newly built, small but
luxurious, and not yet tainted
by pollutants—smog, dust,
sheer corruption—sailing the air
that is life.
A sad place for respite.
To me my parents escaped,
and when they left, what remained—
an emptiness vast and ill-tempered
as typhoon-addled oceans—
stretched and pushed at pristine
walls; my foundation sagged
under heavy vacuity. How
wicked it is to shatter,
become sharp fragments
but not explode.

                                    //

In those sparse woods,
branches naked and taunting,
death crepitating hollowly beneath
naïve feet, I lay still
on his baleful leaf altar.
Small pieces of me carved
out and secreted in painful
dark nooks where demons disguised
as neighbors keep rusted trophies,
dull trinkets, and sorrow.
There I became clay
to be molded, too capricious,
too prosaic to be marble.

//

Words burn like acid,
that much is immutable,
and when burning flesh and blood
sacrifice ceased to suffice,
I found solace in control.
—yearning stomach, eroding teeth!—
Pain and relief knotted
together like some boisterous snatch
of hair which no retching
or guttural sobs could ever free.
On my knees,
head rested exhaustedly
on cool porcelain bowls,
too unencumbered to flush,
I wept.

//

The hospital said: *Watch him.*
I became better at hiding.

//

On that cold quiet night
no clouds bright with old light
behind our former high school
where in the back of Rose's
weathered pale-gold Accord I said
Yes then took it back

But educated fingers held tight
as first love might
to that yes like seatbelts

during a sudden stop
and millions of stars crashed
from the sky and danced
violently behind my eyelids
One by one the old lights
blinked out leaving only Luna
reflecting the sun's derisive
brilliance then a flood
of bright white pain
and she too was gone

//

Under bitter fluorescents,
that unrelenting doctor explained:
poles—his index fingers spread far
apart to drive home meaning,
as if mood dictated intelligence.
To fix your broken thinker
(at this he tapped his left temple)
take one daily.
I asked: *But what of the broken world?*
He stared. I stared.
We stared.
But what of—
Side effects include losing
yourself, and the will to fuck.
Not knowing I could breathe
underwater, I tried drowning
myself instead.

//

Men in uniforms, watchful
of every laugh, acquaintance,
erection, and flies bred
in ptomaine shower drains:
my current species of violence.
Have you *seen* the wriggling
writhing black worms
nourished on disseminated seed,
from which buzzing death blooms?
And so, the broken world
which broke you moves on,
so says the gunslinger,
like an ancient wheel
which navigates sinuous roads
with the finesse of a thousand
ballerinas and scales life's vagaries
with otherworldly ease,

while I become cumflies' feast.
A fitting infestation, indeed.

Notes and Acknowledgments

I would like to thank the editors of the following journals and magazines for publishing poems featured in this collection, some of them from prison, and sometimes in earlier versions:

Evening Street Review—DIY Prison Project: "Under the Courthouse" and "Who Remembers Phone Numbers Anymore?"

Poetry: "These Headphones Should be Free"

reSentencing Volume 2: "Black Enough," "On the Utility of Phone Socks," "Subscribe to Read the Whole Story, or Headline Hoarders" and "Where's the Mail?"

Minutes Before Six: "Salvador :(," "Theoretical Math for DOC Employees," and "The Bathroom Just Smells Better During Late Night, Okay?"

Prison Journalism Project: "Begging" and "Commissary Cuisine Art"

Indiana Review: "Lamentations"

Emergent Literary: "15-Minute Love" and "Basically A Psychologist"

The Shore Poetry: "A Proper Shower"

Union Spring Literary Review: "Hard Work"

Words Beyond Bars: "Little Cup"

Beyond Bars: "Sunset, 7 April 2023"

A huge debt of gratitude to the Willard-Cybulski Correctional Institution Addiction Treatment Unit Staff, who allowed me to make copies free of charge and send out my work. Many thanks to the many inmates who read these poems and gave me feedback. Some of these were inspired by you.

A big thank you to Connor Wolfe, and the team at Wayfarer Books. I may never think my writing is worthy of the world, but at least they do, and they have been so helpful throughout the whole process.

A special thanks to Isaac Pickell who gave this manuscript a much-needed critical eye and made some very helpful and painful suggestions, most of which I applied to this manuscript because they made the poems better.

//

The idea of "writing my wrongs" comes from the title of Shaka Senghor's book *Writing My Wrongs: Life, Death, and Redemption in American Prison.*

The italicized portions of "A Face in Judgment" are lines and phrases borrowed directly from Devin Odell's essay, "A Face in Judgment."

"15-Minute Love" features language borrowed from Lana Del Rey's song "Tulsa Jesus Freak."

The gunslinger referenced in "Personal History Violence" is Roland of Stephen King's epic *Dark Tower* series.

about the author

Kashawn Taylor holds a BA in English and Psychology and an MA in English and Creative Writing. Before his incarceration, he established a strong academic foundation, which he has continued to build upon during his time in prison. His "prison writing" has been featured in several publications, including *Prison Journalism Project*, *The Blotter Magazine*, *Minutes Before Six*, *Evening Street Review's DIY Prison Project*, and *Indiana Review*.

Wayfarer

SINCE 2012

BOOKS

At Wayfarer Books we believe poetry is the language of the earth. We believe words—shaped like rivers through wild places—can change the shape of the world. We publish poets and writers and renegades who stand outside of mainstream culture—poets, essayists, and storytellers whose work might withstand the scrutiny of crows and coyotes, those who are cryptic and floral, the crepuscular, and the queer-at-heart. We are more than just a publisher but a community of writers. Our mission is to produce books that can serve as a compass and map to all wayfarers through wild terrain.

w a y f a r e r b o o k s . o r g

www.ingramcontent.com/pod-product-compliance
Lightning Source LLC
Chambersburg PA
CBHW030459130626
46549CB00007B/2787

9 781965 320280